A Tour Through
Old Lakeland

Guthrie Hutton

Gondola on Coniston Water

Richard Stenlake Publishing
1996

ISBN 1 872074 73 1

First published in the United Kingdom, 1996
By Richard Stenlake Publishing, Ochiltree Sawmill, The Lade,
Ochiltree, Ayrshire, KA18 2NX
Telephone: 01290 423114

Printed by Cordfall Ltd, 0141 332 4640

Sailing on Windermere

INTRODUCTION

For about two hundred years people have been drawn to the unique attractions of the Lake District, but it was not always so. Before the start of the nineteenth century outsiders regarded the mountains as ugly and forbidding, the landscape wet and inhospitable. For locals it was a harsh environment in which to earn a living. Sheep farming was the principal source of employment although mining, quarrying, craft and woodland industries provided work also.

Further back in time Lakelanders endured the extra hazard of living near the Scottish border and the constant threat of raiders, some pursuing ancient grievances, others simply pursuing their neighbours' cattle. In the lawless western marches not all the raiders were Scots; some, owing allegiance to no one and swopping sides for convenience, robbed and pillaged at will until the two countries got together to stop them.

Great castles were useless against such guerilla warriors and so Lakeland's architectural heritage contains few reminders of this once turbulent past; however, it was Lakeland's natural heritage that began to change people's perceptions. Seen in a new and glowing light by William Wordsworth and the other Romantic poets the once threatening mountains and watery landscape became things of beauty. There was a growing appreciation too of wild creatures and flowers and the disorder of natural woodlands.

This change of perception coincided with the development of railways and quite suddenly, from being an unsullied wilderness, the Lake District was threatened by a new and potentially destructive invader. Many of the early railway proposals were aimed at developing mineral resources, bringing jobs and wealth to depressed areas, but many too were aimed at bringing tourists, whose demands on an essentially rural economy would change it forever. Wordsworth and his colleagues, appalled at the prospects, fought hard, with some success, to limit the damage. But the railways and the tourists came and Lakelanders started to cash in on the bonanza.

The influx of visitors brought with it huge dangers for the very landscape and environment the people had come to see. Steamer terminals, holiday homes, hotels and coach roads spread across the country as the Lake District was opened up to ever increasing numbers of people. Many of them came from the industrial north of England but when Manchester Corporation came, it wasn't to enjoy the scenery, it was to build reservoirs for the city. The threat to the area, predicted by Wordsworth, was clear, but so too was the response of a new generation of campaigners who lost the battle to stop the reservoir, but went on to wage war against further damage. The National Trust, founded in 1895, acquired its first property in the Lake District in 1902 and has continued to acquire property ever since. More universal protection was secured by the creation of the Lake District National Park in 1951.

Large numbers of visitors continue to be drawn to the area in all seasons, but with stricter planning controls and almost a quarter of the land in the National Park area now owned by the omnipresent Trust, the Lake District not only survives, but thrives as an island of outstanding scenic beauty. Perhaps it is the variety of what it has to offer that allows it to absorb the pressures of tourism so well – there are mountains to climb, fells to walk, lakes to cruise and a host of museums, pubs and other attractions to tempt the most demanding visitor, just as there was when Victorian and Edwardian tourists started to 'discover' the Lake District. It was always there of course, a landscape as distinctive as the people it nurtured, but Lakelanders are now more likely to win their livelihood in the tourist trade than in the hard, uncertain occupations of their forebears, making it as important for both the visited and the visitor to keep the Lake District special.

Guthrie Hutton

The steamer *Teal* at Bowness

GRASMERE FROM DUNMAIL RAISE.

Eagerly anticipating the delights that lie ahead, a coachload of tourists heads down Dunmail Raise to Grasmere at the turn of the century. On the way, their coach from the Keswick Hotel will dig a little deeper into the ruts on the unmetalled road because a rear wheel has been immobilised by a chain and skid. This was done on steep hills to guard against accidents and give the horses something to pull against.

Dunmail Raise was not always a peaceful tourist route through this beautiful corner of England, indeed it was not always in England. After a tenth century battle here, in which the Cumbrians were defeated by a Northumbrian army, Cumbria became part of Scotland while Lothian was joined to Northumbria (and England). But in the murderous confusion of the time the arrangement did not last, unlike the name of the last Cumbrian King, Dunmail, who lost the battle but gained lasting fame.

The view from the Tea Gardens across the River Rothay to Saint Oswald's church was one of the delights of Grasmere. The view inside the church was another, and it still is. A central wall of double arches supports a complex web of roof trusses, the warm oak contrasting beautifully with the whitewashed walls. The beaten earth floor was originally covered by rushes that were renewed every year in a rushbearing ceremony which continues today, despite the floor being paved in 1840. William Wordsworth and other members of his family are buried in a corner of the churchyard.

One of Grasmere's other delights was (and still is) Sarah Nelson's "celebrated" gingerbread which she made and sold at her cottage cum shop beside the lych gate on the north side of the churchyard. Before it became a gingerbread shop, the cottage was the village school.

A different kind of gingerbread is baked specially and given to the children after the rushbearing ceremony, which is held annually on the nearest Saturday to Saint Oswald's Day, 5th August. Children bearing the rushes (and perhaps dreaming of gingerbread) are seen here outside the church in 1906.

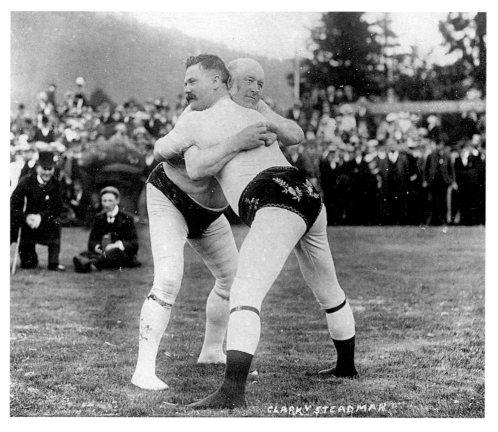

Grasmere Sports grew out of the celebrations surrounding the rushbearing. Initially, it was just a Cumberland wrestling competition, a sport in which wrestlers grasped each other behind the back and tried to 'fall' the opponent by making him lose his footing or grip. George Steadman, the older man facing camera here, was a legend in the sport. He was heavyweight champion numerous times in the late nineteenth century, retiring as champion at the age of 54 after his victory over Hexham Clarke in 1900. Clarke went on to become champion the following year. The pants, worn outside the wrestlers' tights, were not just a style precedent for Superman, there was a prize for the best embroidered decoration too!

Grasmere became Lakeland's premier sports meeting as other sports were added to the wrestling competition. Many were distinctly Lakeland in character, like the race to the top of Butter Crag and back for hill guides. These early athletes were forerunners (forgive the pun) of the modern fell runners who tackle the climb now.

The athletic events were not however confined to running as this picture of a pole vaulter, or pole leaper as he was called, shows. Although the heights were modest by today's standards (10'6" was the winning height in 1900) it was still a long way to drop with neither cushion sole shoes nor a soft pit to land on – this vaulter does not even have the benefit of socks.

Despite numerous other attractions, it is the influence of William Wordsworth that brings so many people to Grasmere. Between 1799 and 1808, Wordsworth and his sister Dorothy lived in Dove Cottage, beside the main turnpike road from Keswick to Ambleside. Here William wrote much of his best work and Dorothy wrote her 'journals', a fascinating and valuable account of contemporary Lakeland life.

A hundred years later Lakeland life had changed. Wealthy Edwardian tourists like these, probably attracted to the area by the image painted by the Wordsworths, and brought by the railways they so vigorously opposed, occupied the Prince of Wales Hotel, across the road from Dove Cottage. The hotel overlooks the little lake of Grasmere although its appeal and that of Wordsworth are perhaps a little lost on the glum looking, sailor-suited, children.

Dick Howe, the Grasmere town crier, or 'bellman', looks rather glum here too; perhaps like the children, he would have preferred a different suit. Or possibly he has just read the news – that could make anyone grumpy!

Around the turn of the century, William Wilson was the proprietor of the Tourist's Rest, a simple stone hut beside Easedale Tarn, where people who ventured up to the tarn could buy something to eat or drink. It was simple fare like bacon and eggs, but while the food itself may have been simple, getting it and the fuel to cook it up to the tarn was not – at least there was plenty of water.

Lines Written on
"Wordsworth's Seat," Rydal,

Whilst on a Walking Tour to Grasmere,
May, 1905.

Not to seek for inspiration,
　Do I thus these steps ascend ;
But to stay the perspiration,
　Which in copious drops descend.

Tired, footsore, weak and weary,
　Here I've come at last to rest ;
Though alone I am not dreary,
　For the scene is at its best.

Here I sit and think of Wordsworth,
　Poet of the Lake and Fell ;
For each brook, and wood, and moorland,
　Had for him a magic spell.

Rydal's waters lave before me,
　Knabb Scarr's crags they frown behind ;
Loughrigg's summit—Rothay's murmur,
　Bring the poet to my mind.

Place of ever-changing beauty,
　In all seasons of the year ;
Ever vernal, ever lovely,
　And to me for ever dear.

13, Calton Terrace, 　　　William Troughton.
　Morecambe.

Note.—A copy of the above has been most graciously accepted by Mrs. Wordsworth, of Rydal Mount.

Wordsworth moved to Rydal in 1813 and lived there until his death in 1850. Half a century later his influence continued to inspire others, like William Troughton of Morecambe. He penned these wonderfully un-Wordsworthian lines while sitting on 'Wordsworth's seat', a large rock overlooking Rydal Water where the great man was reputed to have sat. The busy A591 now passes so close to what is left of the rock that all a poet could contemplate from it today is the volume of traffic.

Between Rydal and Ambleside a public footpath leads from the A591 across a field to the River Rothay where it crosses these 'hipping', or stepping, stones, carefully set a pace apart and shaped with a pointed edge to break the water.

Like Saint Oswald's in Grasmere, Saint Mary's church at Ambleside has retained the traditions of an annual rushbearing ceremony. It takes place on the first Saturday in July when the 'bearings' are paraded through the town. The centrepiece of the parade is a decorated harp, the Harp of David, seen on the right of this picture from the early 1900s. The old Saint Mary's church was replaced in 1854 by the present building designed by the eminent Victorian architect, Sir George Gilbert Scott.

Ambleside hotels were ideally placed to cash in on the Victorian and Edwardian demand for touring as seen here with carriages loading up outside two of the oldest hotels, the Salutation and the White Lion. Trips radiated in all directions, to Coniston, Langdale, Keswick and over the Kirkstone Pass to Ullswater. There were local Ambleside attractions too, like the waterfall known as Stock Ghyll Force (a sign to the right of the White Lion directs travellers to it). The early car to the left of the White Lion however is a sign of the way touring would change and in the bottom picture, from around 1930, the motor car has replaced the horse. Hill's Vale View, now the Churchill Hotel, is on the left and the White Lion is in the background.

Ambleside is set back from the northern end of Windermere and so Waterhead Pier, seen here with carriages meeting the steamer *Swift* (above), is about a mile from the town centre.

Windermere Lake, Ambleside Pier.

The steamer *Tern* is seen here (left) alongside the pier. She was a twin screw steam yacht, built at Wyvenhoe in Essex and introduced to Lake service in 1891. She survived the economic unheavals of two world wars, although during the Second World War she was used as a naval training ship and renamed HMS *Undine*. Assuming her old name after the war, she was converted to diesel in the 1950s and is still a favourite with visitors to the lake today.

The *Tern* was joined on the lake in the 1930s by two 250 ton motor cruisers which perpetuated the names of earlier lake steamers. The *Teal* (bottom right), launched in 1936, and the *Swan* (bottom left) of 1938 were built in Barrow and transported by rail in sections to be reassembled on the lake. Both are still in service.

The "Teal" at Waterhead, Windermere.

Cumbria figured prominently in the development of marine flying and the first British attempts to take off and land an aircraft on water took place in 1910 and 1911 on Windermere. One aircraft failed to take off, another crash-landed, but a third, an aircraft called *Waterbird*, completed the first successful flight. The landing wheels of the monoplane seen here on Windermere have been replaced by a single float known as a broad-beam scow, an arrangement favoured for many early 'hydro-aeroplanes'. The first twin float system was pioneered at Barrow-in-Furness and later, during the Second World War, Sunderland Flying boats were built at Troutbeck Bridge (now White Cross Bay) where the caravan park and chalet site is today.

Here a twin float bi-plane flies over Waterhead as the more traditional means of lake transport, the steamer *Swift*, departs from the pier. To the right is a photograph of the *Swift* taken from one of these early aircraft.

Wray Castle, built in the 1840s on the north western shore of Lake Windermere, is a Victorian Gothic pile with little sham ruins, like the one behind this passive oarsman, scattered around the grounds. It was here, while on holiday with her family, that Beatrix Potter grew to love the Lake District countryside and its wild creatures. In 1929 Wray Castle was given to the National Trust to protect the lake shore.

At only fifteen feet high, Skelwith Force on the River Brathay is one of the lesser waterfalls in the Lake District, but what it lacks in height it makes up for by having the greatest volume of any fall in the area. The placid river changes character as it hurtles between these narrow jaws of rock, diving and twisting into the roaring cauldron below, a scene that has clearly inspired this artist to capture it on canvas and our photographer to commit it to film.

Geological formations have provided the Langdale Valley with the most distinctive mountain scenery in the Lake District. They have also provided the local people with work. Slate quarries like Thrang at Chapel Stile and the larger Elterwater were both once worked extensively, but are now just scars on the hillsides with only abandoned spoil heaps remaining as reminders of the valley's industrial past.

At the head of Great Langdale, at Wall End Farm, was a hutted holiday centre belonging to the Holiday Fellowship. It had a communal living room and kitchen in a large hut, and sleeping accommodation in smaller huts alongside. Such simple pleasures meant a lot to people who could otherwise not afford a holiday in the country, but the huts were removed in the 1960s.

Of all the fearsome Lakeland passes, Kirkstone Pass between Windermere and Ullswater was perhaps the one most early tourists wanted to cross. At 1500 feet this was a seriously high pass and the thrill of attempting such a dangerous journey (in the company of an experienced driver, of course) was not to be missed. Often, however, passengers had to get out to lighten the load and sometimes give the coach a shove to help the horses. Here a string of carriages ascend the steepest stretch from the Ullswater side, with Brothers Water in the distance.

Of the two routes up from Windermere, the one from Ambleside is the steepest and is aptly known as 'The Struggle'. Here a four-in-hand coach heading for Ullswater is being helped up the hill by a pair with an outrider – a bit like a banking engine helping a railway train on a steep gradient.

Despite the ease with which modern traffic negotiates the pass, the Kirkstone Inn is still a popular stopping-off place for tourists. It even has three rooms with four-poster beds. There has been an inn on the site catering for passing travellers since 1496. It expanded in the late eighteenth century when stagecoaches started to use the newly improved road and really came into its own when Victorian and Edwardian tourists discovered the delights of Lake District coaching. However, in the horse drawn days, a rest at the inn was not just well earned, it was often a necessity. The inn's location at 'Top o' Kirkstone' was, and still is, very remote and the lower picture, looking towards Windermere, beautifully conveys the empty stillness that descends on such a place when the noise of the last coach party dies away.

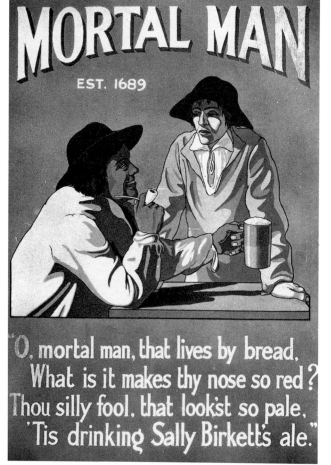

Between Kirkstone Pass and Windermere is the straggling village of Troutbeck where this "old cottage", known as Town End farm is situated. The first part of the house was built in 1626 by George Browne and it remained in the Browne family until 1942 when it was given to the National Trust. Across the road from the dwelling house is the wool barn and spinning gallery. The Brownes were yeomen sheep farmers, known in these parts as 'statesmen', part of an emerging rural middle class in the seventeenth and early eighteenth centuries.

Among Troutbeck's other claims to fame is the Mortal Man Inn, and its original sign. Apparently painted in order to pay his bar bill, the artist responsible for the sign was Julius Caesar Ibbotson who once lived at Troutbeck. It showed the pallid puritan Ned Partridge and the jovial beer drinker Nat Fleming exchanging some philosphical words. Ibbotson's sign has long gone, but the message is as clear as ever – cheers!

This postcard of Major and Mrs Noble on the steps of Calgarth Hall may have been used by the Major as campaign material during the North Westmorland by-election in 1905. Major Noble stood for the Conservatives but despite reducing their majority to 220 votes he lost to Liberal's Mr Lief Jones. The experience must have put him off politics because he did not contest the general election the following year. His successor, Lord Kerry also lost to Mr Jones, but this time by only three votes.

The old coaching inn of Low Wood, between Ambleside and Windermere, is now one of the largest hotels in Lakeland with a water sports centre on the foreshore instead of this lone fisherman. However, it all might have been very different. The Kendal and Windermere Railway Company proposed to terminate their line from Oxenholme at Low Wood, but they ran into furious opposition from William Wordsworth and others who feared that the railway's ultimate intention was to continue the line through the Vale of Grasmere to Keswick

In the face of such opposition, the railway company made a tactical retreat, proposing a new terminus further south at the hamlet of Birthwaite, a mile from the lake shore. Wordsworth continued to object, but with the threat to the Vale of Grasmere removed, the railway was approved. It opened in April 1847 and ran to a station called Windermere, beginning a gradual process whereby Birthwaite's name disappeared from common usage to be replaced by Windermere. People came in ever increasing numbers, fulfilling Wordsworth's prediction that the railway would change the area, but now the railway itself has changed – only a single line platform remains and a supermarket has replaced this extensive canopied terminus.

One 'Poet Laureate', however, was happy that the railway had penetrated the Lake District – John Close, also known as "Poet Laureate to His Majesty the King of Grand Bonny, Western Africa". Every summer from 1864 to the turn of the century, 'Poet Close' arrived from Kirkby Stephen to set himself up at Bowness in his 'Sentry' or 'Pigeon Box' where he tried to tempt visitors to buy books of his eccentric verse.

Like Birthwaite, Bowness was irrevocably changed by the railway. Travellers, whose means or available time did not allow them to venture far from the station, swamped Bowness and transformed it from an ancient fishing village in a sheltered inland bay to a steamer terminal and lakeside resort. Windermere and Bowness quickly merged into one community as new buildings catering for the tourist market sprang up – the building this horse-drawn bus is passing was a bank and the picture was taken from the balcony of the Royal Hotel.

New hotels were among the more obvious developments caused by tourism and one of the most conspicuous was the Royal. Now shorn of its ornate first floor balcony, it is seen here in all its early glory. The passengers in the foreground are boarding coaches bound in opposite directions, Coniston and Ullswater.

The First World War took the gloss off the tourist trade, but inspired everybody to do their patriotic duty, including this group in Bowness sewing sand bags for the front. They and the little old cannon beside them are a world away from the appalling horrors of the front and the large calibre howitzers their sandbags would soon be protecting soldiers from.

One visitor to the Lakes during the war was Major-General Sir Robert Baden-Powell, founder of the Boy Scout movement. He came to inspect the Westmorland Scouts in August 1915 and some, like the Kirkby Stephen troop who cycled to Windermere, came a long way to meet him. After the inspection and tea the 1st Windermere Sea Scouts rowed Sir Robert and Lady Baden-Powell in their gig, *Sea Otter*, from Bowness to Mere Garth where they put on a display of swimming and diving for their guests.

Perch fishing on Windermere has gone on for many years as this early twentieth century picture shows. At one time there were numerous small Perch in the lake, but they were fished extensively during the Second World War and canned as a sardine substitute called 'perchines'. Disease almost wiped out the remaining population in the 1970s, giving their natural predators, the Pike, a feeding problem which they solved by attacking the Char, a trout-like fish unique to the Lake District and thought to be a survivor from the ice age.

Brief 'ice ages' have occasionally returned to Windermere. In February 1907 the lake froze from Bowness across to Belle Isle, encouraging skaters to test its strength and the District Council to place ladders on the boat piers in case of accidents. The ice continued south of Bowness but the steamers apparently ruined the prospect of the southern lake becoming an unbroken sheet of ice.

The pier became the focal point of the lakeside at Bowness, with boat hiring jetties occupying the bay beside it. Here the steamer *Swift* backs in alongside the pier, a manoeuvre still practised by the boats today.

Swift was built in 1900 and continued as a steamer until 1956 when she was converted to diesel. She was later withdrawn from service and further converted for use as a floating exhibition centre. *Swift* was built by T.B. Seath of Rutherglen, near Glasgow who specialised in building craft in sections for reassembly on inland navigations. The lower pictures show her in her early steam days.

One of Seath's earlier steamers, the *Swan*, was the first screw-propelled boat on the lake, which had hitherto been the preserve of paddle steamers. She is seen here leaving Lakeside for Bowness.

Swan went into service in 1869 and was joined on the lake ten years later by these two similar but smaller boats, *Teal* and *Cygnet* (Left). They were built in sections at Barrow and brought by rail to Lakeside where they were reassembled. Both survived the First World War, but *Teal* was withdrawn in 1927 while *Cygnet* was re-engined and continued in service up to the Second World War. Plans to take her to Ullswater after the war came to nought and she was finally broken up in those scrap-happy days of the 1960s.

Windermere has always presented a formidable barrier between Kendal and the busy villages of the Furness fells and so, to meet the needs of east-west traffic, a ferry has crossed the lake for centuries. The early boats were powered by nothing more sophisticated than a set of oars, but despite this carts and small carriages like Broughams could squeeze on board the larger of two boats. With the horses sandwiched between the vehicles and bits of cart projecting precariously beyond the sides of the wooden boat it was something of a tight fit.

As the size and number of carts and carriages increased, the old rowing boats could not cope and were replaced in 1870 by this steam ferry. It could, as seen here, take a fully loaded four-in-hand coach with the passengers still in their seats and the horses still in the shafts. Although the original purpose of the ferry was to meet the needs of east-west traffic, the new ferry became part of a popular tourist route for coaches taking in Coniston and the central Lakes.

756. The ferry boat on Windermere.

Unlike its muscle-powered predecessor, the steam ferry was kept in line by cables laid on the bed of the lake. It used the cables to pull itself across the lake as did this diesel successor which replaced it in 1915. The cables and guide pulleys can be clearly seen in the pictures on these two pages. The same system of cable propulsion has continued to be used by subsequent ferries such as the *Drake*, introduced in 1954, and the present boat, the *Mallard*, which was commissioned in March 1990. The crossing must now be the smoothest and most relaxing car journey in the Lake District, but it was not always trouble free. In 1635 an overloaded boat capsized and sank, drowning forty-seven people returning from a wedding at Hawkshead (who are buried in a communal grave at Saint Martin's Parish Church, Bowness). A number of horses also perished in the disaster.

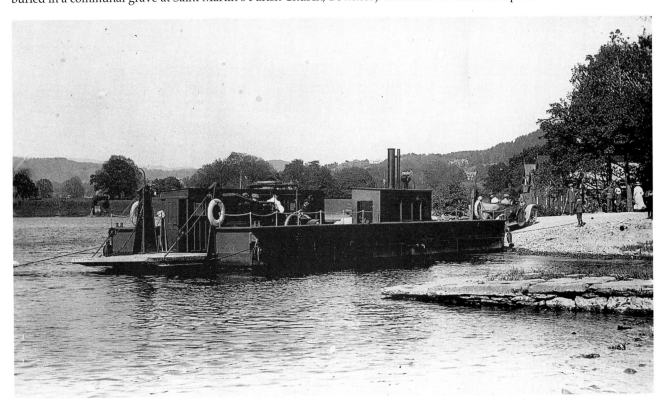

The steam ferry must have made life a lot easier for carters like the Robinson Brothers whose cart is shown in the top picture. They operated between the Bowness area and Kendal while Ellwoods, who operated the cart in the lower picture, worked between Kendal and the towns and villages of Cartmel. Before carters started to appear on Lakeland roads in the 1750s, most goods were transported by pack horses. Packhorse routes radiated from Kendal to all parts of the Lake District and the 'auld grey town' was also a centre for packhorse traffic between the north of England and Scotland. These tough beasts could carry prodigious loads in their panniers and negotiate mountain passes that have since fallen into disuse. Improvements to the roads in the 1750s and '60s saw the packhorses gradually replaced by carts. The new roads, known as turnpikes after their toll gates, also encouraged the development of stagecoaches.

Buses eventually replaced stagecoaches on Cumbrian roads. This early vehicle is heading south along Milnthorpe Road in Kendal; behind is the Nether Bridge and Kendal Parish Church. To the left of the picture is the house where the artist George Romney lived until his death in 1802. Kendal's position as the southern gateway to the Lake District, with easy access to the markets of the south, made it a natural centre for the wool trade. Cloth was woven on hand looms and socks were knitted by hand before mills powered by the River Eden and its tributaries took the town into the industrial age.

Many of the pictures in this book, including this one, are old picture postcards from the days when a half-penny stamp would guarantee same-day delivery. Now fax machines, telephones and 'E-mail' compete with the successors of these Kendal postmen setting out on their morning delivery from Finkle Street. The present Post Office, opposite the library in Stricklandgate, was opened in 1930.

When the Furness Railway Company opened its line from Carnforth to Barrow in 1846, it also laid on coaches to take passengers from Dalton to the steamer pier at Newby Bridge. Not content with that, they set about building a railway from Greenodd to the lake, but instead of stopping it at Newby Bridge, they moved the terminus and pier to Lakeside, where the steamers would have more room to manoeuvre. The line was opened in June 1869.

The railway terminal, with its the distinctive tower, was located alongside the pier giving passengers the shortest possible walk between train and steamer. However, the railway didn't put all of its energies into tourism but also extended its goods and carrying services onto the lake with the cargo boat *Raven* (above right). She started work in 1871 and is now exhibited at the Windermere Steamboat Museum. Behind her, *Swift* is seen easing away from the pier while *Tern* sits alongside. Below, the *Tern* heads away from the pier.

The early steamers were operated by the Windermere United Steam Yacht Company which had been formed in 1858 by the merger of two early rivals; however, the company's independence was short lived. The railway company, anxious to control what it saw as an essential tourist operation, bought shares in the steamer company and a few years later bought the company itself. It quickly started to improve the fleet, first with the *Swan*, then *Teal* and *Cygnet*, and in 1900, *Swift*.

Much has changed over the years. *Swift*, shown above in her glory days approaching the pier, is now an engineless hulk and the station buildings, along with the ornate canopy above the balcony have gone. For a while the railway too was closed but in 1973 the Lake Side to Haverthwaite section was brought back to life, reviving and continuing for future generations a sense of what it must have been like for our Victorian forebears to arrive beside the lake by train. Then, as in the lower picture, to experience that frisson of excitement as the mooring lines are slipped and the steamer eases away from the pier to sail into the delights of a Lakeland holiday.

Lakeside was not all piers, steamers and railway stations, although attracting tourists was still the main purpose of the refreshment rooms in the lodge beside the Jubilee Institute. The lodge was built in 1899, twelve years after the institute itself which is hidden behind the tree here on the left.

Windermere ceases to be a lake and becomes the River Leven at Newby Bridge. 'Leven' is a Celtic word meaning Elm and it is a curious co-incidence that England's largest lake and Scotland's largest loch, Loch Lomond, are both drained by rivers called Leven. Beside the seventeenth century bridge that gives the village its name is the eighteenth century Swan Hotel. Here patrons are taking tea on its riverside terrace shaded by this impressive pergola.

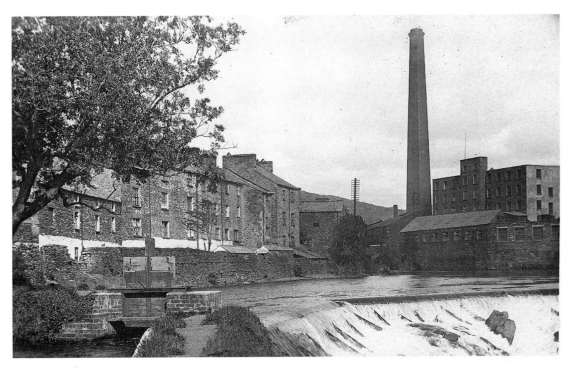

The Leven's rapid fall at Backbarrow encouraged the development of the industry that was the antithesis of the poets' romantic image of the Lake District. The gaunt mills in the background (now the centre of a timeshare complex) notoriously exploited child labour to produce cotton and were later used to make make washing blue. The weir and sluice in the foreground however were part of the industry that brought Backbarrow early industrial fame. The first charcoal-fired cold blast-furnace was established here in 1711 and close by was Isaac Wilkinson's pioneering iron works.

Isaac's son, John, who took over the Backbarrow iron works from his father, had such a passion for all things iron that he became known as 'Iron mad Wilkinson'. He lived at Lindale-in-Cartmel and is commemmorated there by an iron obelisk beside the road to Grange. He is buried in an iron coffin in Lindale churchyard. Lindale is built on hills where the main road here rises steeply out of the village to the west. Over the years the road became very busy before the new by-pass was needed to restore it to something like its former self.

Although Backbarrow's iron works were part of the emerging industrial revolution its charcoal fuel was derived from the ancient woodland industry of Furness, coppicing. Coppices were areas of woodland where trees were allowed to grow to the required size before being cut, and once cut allowed to regenerate before being cropped again. Farm animals browsed the woodland floor to keep it clear of unwanted growth.

The best wood for making charcoal was oak, birch, alder or hazel, although one Lakeland industry, gunpowder making, preferred charcoal made from juniper. It was made by the controlled burning of a carefully-laid pile of poles and branches under a covering of earth and grass which had to be kept intact as the pile shrank. At the end of the burn the charcoal had to be damped down; too much water and the charcoal was soft, too little and it all went up in flames. On average, it took seven tons of wood to produce one ton of charcoal.

It was more economical for charcoal to be produced on site and so while they were working charcoal burners lived in the woods in these turf-roofed conical huts. The appearance of the huts and the life of the charcoal burners will be familiar to readers of Arthur Ransome's children's adventure story, Swallows and Amazons.

Coppices produced wood for a variety of woodworking crafts and these woodcutters at Backbarrow could be preparing for any one of them. The strips of wood could be hoops for wooden barrels – coopering was one Lakeland craft, another was making cart wheels – perhaps the cart is in for repair, or maybe the semi-circle of benches suggests that they are basket makers, or swillers.

This rogues gallery of swillers could have been based anywhere in the Furness area, but since the picture was used as a postcard from Haverthwaite they may have have been photographed there. The swill is an oval basket made from oak which is boiled, softened, cut into strips and woven onto a hoop of hazel. It was mainly used for gathering potatoes but was also adapted for other industries including cockle gathering in Morecambe Bay.

Bobbin making was another woodland industry that developed in response to the huge expansion of the Lancashire cotton mills in the nineteenth century. The mills needed a vast number of bobbins and the Lake District, with its extensive coppices and abundant water power, was well placed to provide them. This belt-driven travelling saw bench is typical of the water-powered machinery in these mills.

To begin with bobbins were made in old mills adapted for the purpose, but as the demand grew new mills were erected – Stott Park was one of these. It was purpose built near Finsthwaite by local landowner John Harrison and went into production in 1836. Birch was the favoured wood for bobbins but as new synthetic materials became available, demand for wooden bobbins and cotton reels diminished. Some mills diversified into other wood-turned products like tool handles and rollers, and Stott Park continued in this way up to its closure in 1971. It has now been reopened as a working museum. In this typical image from an early twentieth century bobbin mill, a blocking machine operator works in a snowdrift of wood dust.

LAKE COUNTRY INDUST
BLOCKING MACHINE.

The new A590 road cut the Lakeside railway north of Haverthwaite, limiting the section of line that could be restored, but in 1932 it was the railway that briefly closed the road. An engine pulling two waggons and pushing ten to Backbarrow failed to go over a hill and was pushed back out of control through Haverthwaite. It crashed through stop blocks and a wall, ending up in this spectacular heap across the road. Miraculously, no one was hurt and railway traffic was unaffected because the train had left the rails through a siding. However, the road was blocked for some hours – an effective, if risky way to deal with the competition!

Recent improvements to Lakeland roads have been argued over in the same way that the early railway proposals were, but whether building new roads or repairing old, those unsung heroes, the navvies, have to turn out in all weathers to do it. Here a gang of men, believed to be in the Lindale area, are busy – having a break!

Grizedale Beck flows past Satterthwaite, taking a pronounced S-bend beneath this bridge which was re-built in 1905 as part of general road and bridge improvements in the area. Below, the bridge builders pose proudly with some of their machinery beside their finished work. Satterthwaite village is in the background. It is now surrounded by the 'unnatural' Grizedale Forest which is the source of much soul searching for those anxious to retain the purity of the Lake District landscape – although the much managed coppice woods are of course 'unnatural' too!

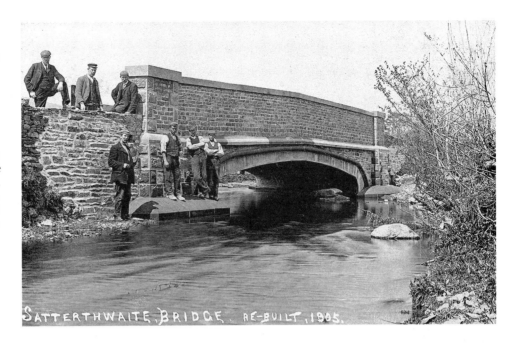

SATTERTHWAITE BRIDGE. RE-BUILT 1905.

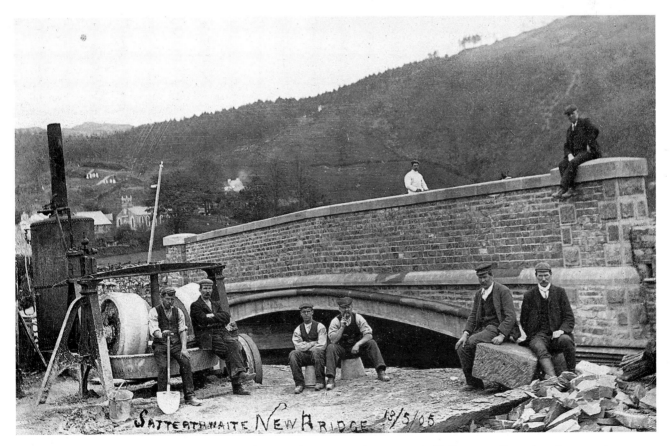

SATTERTHWAITE NEW BRIDGE 18/5/05

Author's aside: On at least one occasion, I too have wished Grizedale Forest would disappear. I was fourth runner in an orienteering relay team of seven that was laced with Internationalists and included one former World Cup winner. The event was the Harvester Trophy Relays of 1990 and I took over with our team in front. I lost the lead, regained it, lost it again and handed over in second place. Our next runner (the World Cup winner) re-established our lead, but we slipped back again to finish a very close second. The unique thing about the 'Harvester' is that it takes place at night and my run through Grizedale was between 3 and 4 o'clock on a very dark morning. Oh yes, I remember Grizedale – by lamp light!

Hawkshead might have been built for an exhibition or a film set, but this compact cluster of buildings and narrow streets is real and quite unique. Flag Street, seen here, is one of the main streets. It has a small beck flowing between the houses, below the flagstone paving and under the large hole in the foreground that gave the villagers access to it (but would give today's average health and safety inspector apoplexy!). At the time of this picture Hawkshead was a working village engaged mainly in the wool trade, but now the beck has been culverted under neat geometric slabs and the lived-in character of these houses has been lost under a coat of pristine whitewash. Tourists are the main trade now.

Grandy Neuk is another quaint corner of Hawkshead adjacent to the lodgings where it is believed William Wordworth stayed when he attended Hawkshead Grammer School.

Hawkshead had a number of inns and three of them have been home to the 'Girt Clog'. It was made for a John Watterson whose left foot became so badly swollen by a condition, believed to have been elephantitis, that he feared it would stop him working and he would starve or end up in the poor house. So local cobbler, John Rigg, made this enormous clog for him. It was 20 inches long, 16 inches across and 7 inches high at the heel. When Watterson died, his widow gave the clog to the Brown Cow Inn which, she claimed, had seen more of him than she had. The right picture shows the clog at the Brown Cow, but when it closed the clog was moved to the Kings Arms and it is now in the Queen's Head.

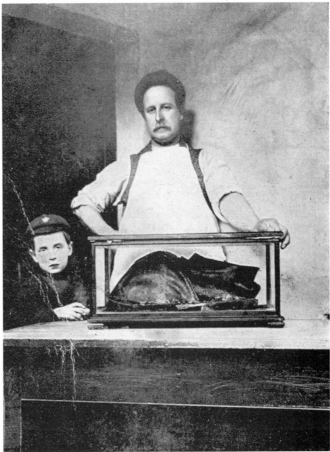

Another of Hawkshead's inns, the Red Lion, is seen to the left behind this coach taking on passengers for Windermere and Coniston. The building on the right is now the National Trust's Beatrix Potter Gallery. It was formerly used as an office by her husband, William Heelis.

The primary purpose of the Coniston Railway was to serve the copper mines and quarries above Coniston. It was originally run as an independent line but was taken over by the Furness Railway in 1862. Its route was not very 'tourist friendly'. It joined the Furness Railway at Foxfield and headed north past Woodland and Torver to terminate on the high ground above Coniston village. This alignment, with the terminus some distance from the shore and veering away from the lake, proved to be the line's ultimate undoing because when the mines and quarries finished production it was not well placed to cater for tourists. It closed for passengers in 1958 and for goods in 1962. The top picture shows the railmotor train, which was introduced to the branch line around 1905, at Foxfield. Below is Woodland Station around the same time.

One of the fiercest critics of the railway, the line it took and its effect on the local population, was John Ruskin. He was one of the foremost thinkers of his day and his opposition must have been a severe embarrassment to the railway company. He lived on the east side of the lake at Brantwood and would have been familiar with this almost unchanged view of Coniston village from the church gate. To the right is the sixteenth century Black Bull Hotel and to the left is the Bridge House Cafe, positioned behind the bridge over Church Beck.

Church Beck flows out of Coppermines Valley, where nearly three quarters of Lake District copper was mined before the end of the nineteenth century. An attempt to recover material from the old spoil heaps petered out before the First World War, but the former office and manager's office lived on as a youth hostel, as described on the back of this card: "A climb into the heart of the hills about one and a half miles from the village. Very bleak but oh! what comfort within. Blazing fires, piano, violin and by far the best cooking and supply of eatables. Every convenience for drying wet clothes etc. Road metal still made here, but copper mines exhausted."

The *Gondola* arrived on Coniston in 1859. She was built at Liverpool in sections and assembled on the shore at Coniston Hall. Her arrival coincided with the completion of the Coniston Railway but since that coincided with the slow demise of the workable copper ores, the railway had to rely more heavily than expected on her appeal to tourists. They were not to be disappointed, because, despite the geographical difficulties, *Gondola*'s graceful, distinctive lines attracted large numbers of visitors and ensured that she stayed in service up to 1937. Her boiler was sold, but she survived as an engineless houseboat until the early 1960s when she became stranded during a storm. Wrecked, but not forgotten, this most distinctive of all Lakes steamers was rescued and restored by the National Trust and started cruising again in 1980.

Gondola's popularity, in those halcyon Edwardian summers before the First World War, was such that when the Furness Railway tried to replace her, they couldn't. The boat they had intended to take her place was *Lady of the Lake*. She was built in Southampton and like all lake steamers taken in bits and assembled on the lake shore from where she was launched in 1908. Despite her unusual canoe-like curved bow and railway engine-like funnel she was unable to replace *Gondola* in people's affections and so the two boats operated on the lake together until *Gondola* was sold in 1937. *Lady of the Lake* continued on her own up to the outbreak of the Second World War but was laid up for its duration and never went back into service. She was broken up in 1950.

The world water speed record was broken eleven times during the 1930s and on four of those occasions the record breaker was Sir Malcolm Campbell (who also broke the world land speed record nine times). His first three records were set in Italy and Switzerland, but in August 1939, two weeks before the outbreak of the Second World War, he raced his *Bluebird II* across Coniston Water at a speed of 141.74 mph, a record that stood throughout the war years.

After the war Campbell resolved not to let the Americans beat his 'British' world record. He replaced *Bluebird*'s conventional engine with a 4,000 horse-power jet engine and had a new streamlined superstructure built around it. The re-built boat, however, shown in the above pictures arriving at Coniston in June 1947, proved unstable at high speed and despite modifications, failed to break the record. It was Sir Malcom's last attempt on either the land or water speed record as he died the following year.

After Sir Malcolm's death his son, Donald, took up the challenge. In 1955 he broke the record and the magical 200 mph barrier on Ullswater with a new *Bluebird*. He broke it again, twice overseas and four times on Coniston, where he is seen celebrating his 225.63 mph triumph of 1956. He returned to Coniston in November 1966 with a new turbo-jet engine in *Bluebird*, but was unable to make the attempt until 4th January 1967. On the first run his speed was 297 mph, but a record is the average of two runs and on the second the bow lifted, the boat crashed and Campbell was killed. The record could not be ratified.

Sir Henry Seagrave and one of his two mechanics also died in a speed record attempt on Windermere in 1930. The average of the first two runs was 98.76 mph, but the boat crashed as they attempted to break the 100mph barrier on a third run, unofficially timed at 119.8 mph. Their more conventional looking speedboat, *Miss England II*, is here surrounded by an expectant throng before the fatal attempt.

In an area dominated by Norse place names, the Penn, the prominent hill here, and Logan Beck in front of it, have unmistakable Celtic origins. The Beck is a tributary of the Duddon, joining it a mile north of Duddon Bridge.

Further up the Duddon Valley is Seathwaite church, made famous by its parson, Robert Walker. His wide ranging ministrations to his flock between 1735 and 1802 earned him the epithet, 'Wonderful Walker'. He taught the children and healed the sick, sheared sheep and spun the wool, wove cloth and tanned leather – seemingly there was no limit to his endeavours. He even made furniture and one of his chairs is still in the church which was re-built in 1874 and is seen here from across Tarn Beck

The peaceful little village of Seathwaite would no doubt only ever have found fame by its tiny church, but, on 25th July 1904, the demon drink intervened. Some men from the Barrow waterworks site at Seathwaite Tarn were drinking in the Newfield Inn when one man was refused more drink. After a heated argument he and his mates were ejected, but, under a hail of stones, they forced their way back into the bar which they raided and wrecked. They then moved on to smash windows at the vicarage and church before returning to attack the little hotel again. The terrified landlord, his barman and an engineer from the water-works had barricaded themselves inside, armed with shotguns. The rioters responded to a warning by intensifying their attack and so the three men opened fire. Three rioters were shot, one died soon after and another lost his leg a month later. Peace has since returned to Seathwaite!

The agricultural show is an institution. It gives farmers a chance to show off their stock and, perhaps just as importantly, get together for a good crack. Here sheep are being shown at the Eskdale Show in 1935, a year apparently marked by the appearance for the first and only time of Swaledale sheep brought across to the west from an Ullswater farm.

The other Lakeland institution that gives farmers the opportunity to indulge in a spot of socialising is the hunt. Fox hunting takes place in the hill sheep country from winter through to lambing time in spring. The rugged Cumbrian hills however are no place for red coated horsemen, the huntsmen here are farmers protecting their sheep and the hunting is done on foot, sometimes covering prodigious distances in pursuit of a fox. Here the Eskdale and Ennerdale hounds search amongst rocks that could give the fox ideal cover or trap a chasing hound.

The meeting of the three old Lake District counties at the top of Wrynose Pass was originally marked by three boulders, but they were replaced in the nineteenth century by the Three Shire Stone. The stone was the creation of a passionate Lancastrian, William Field of Cartmel, who had it carved with "Lancashire" on one side and "WF 1816" on the other. Thus complete, or rather incomplete because it didn't have Cumberland and Westmorland on it, it lay until after Field's death in 1860 when his surviving relatives carried out his original intention and erected the stone.

Bracken, that creeping scourge of hill and moorland grazing, was put to good use by Lakeland famers who cut it as winter bedding for cattle and horses. Here a Boot hill farmer leads a heavy load cart of cut bracken through the Eskdale hills.

The Ravenglass and Eskdale Railway was opened in 1875 to bring heamatite ore out from the mines at Boot. Passenger services started the following year after improvements were made to the track. When the mines failed in 1882, passengers became the main source of income and the line struggled on until after a series of closures and re-starts it finally ground to a halt in 1913. New owners took it over two years later and proceeded to reduce the original 3' 0" gauge to 15" while progressively re-opening the line; they also closed the terminus at Boot and established a new one at Dalegarth. The line was taken over again in 1949 but was back on the market and heading for oblivion by the late 1950s when the Ravenglass and Eskdale Railway Preservation Society stepped in to save it. Numerous improvements later, the Lake District's most endearing railway has also proved to be its most enduring. The top picture shows the old Boot terminus with the original 3' 0" gauge passenger train, below is the 15" gauge replacement.

Gosforth, on the western edge of the National Park and only a short distance from the sea, is a village with strong Norse influences. The name itself is Norse in origin and means 'goose ford', but the main claim to fame is a slender stone cross in Saint Mary's churchyard which is carved with a mixture of Norse and early Christian symbols.

The people living on this narrow road leading down from Hardingill to the village square are now served (if that's the right word) by double decker buses that fill the road. The houses facing on the right have been knocked into one with the right hand door now a window. The Globe Inn is just out of picture to the right.

Gosforth's other church is the Methodist Church, built in 1874 and seen here on the right. The road to Nether Wasdale and Wasdale Head leads off to the left, in front of the house with the distinctive round-topped gable window.

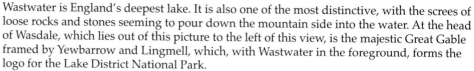

Wastwater is England's deepest lake. It is also one of the most distinctive, with the screes of loose rocks and stones seeming to pour down the mountain side into the water. At the head of Wasdale, which lies out of this picture to the left of this view, is the majestic Great Gable framed by Yewbarrow and Lingmell, which, with Wastwater in the foreground, forms the logo for the Lake District National Park.

Wasdale Head was the cradle of rock climbing which developed from the rock scrambling of earlier generations into a serious sport towards the end of the nineteenth century. It changed the fortunes of the Wastwater Hotel, now the Wasdale Head Inn. Climbers made it their own, as this picture of boots and climbing equipment in the entrance hall indicates. They relaxed by indulging in various tests of skill such as traversing the barn or the underside of the billiard table.

The Summit

They traversed the real thing on fearsome rock formations like Scafell Crag, seen here from Mickeldore, an igneous intrusion that has weathered into the well defined gap between Scafell and the neighbouring peak of Scafell Pike. Scafell is the parent mountain, but at 3162 feet above sea level, the Pike is the highest mountain in England.

The little cartoons on these two pages, under the heading "Having a drop o' Summit", are one cartoonist's idea of the real purpose of "Climbing in Lakeland". Maybe he would have been more respectful if he had attempted Scafell Crag himself!

THE GABLE TRAVERSE

Coming Down

Facing Wasdale, below the summit of Great Gable are the Napes Ridges, a climber's paradise of rock aretes that to ordinary mortals (like me) are terrifying just to look at, let alone climb. This traverse below the ridges leads to the Napes' ultimate challenge, the Needle. It was first climbed in 1886 by W.P. Haskett-Smith who wrote his name into the history books of the sport when he scaled it alone and without the aid of ropes or "other illegitimate means"! He left a handkercheif on top as proof of his feat.

Many of the Napes rock formations have been given names to match their appearance, like the Sphinx Rock (that looks more like an Easter Island monolith), and this, appropriately dubbed Arrowhead Ridge.

A lone climber stands on top of the Needle with his colleagues strung out below – count them, there are more than at first glance and surely too many to stand on the top together, unless they were also making an attempt on the Guinness Book of Records.

One great climb, that once had no name, is shown in the top two pictures. The Innominate Crack is one of two fissures that challenge some climbers to tackle the 60 foot high buttress of Kern Knotts. The other, to the left, is unexcitingly called Kern Knotts Crack which was first climbed in 1897.

To the right is a feature known as the Eagle's Nest, presumably because access to it by wing is infinitely preferable to doing it on foot. This part of the climb was described in the original caption to this picture as "The Difficult Bit" (get away!).

Great Gable can be done the easy way too (although easy is a relative term for any 2949 foot mountain). This group of walkers, in skirts, suits and carrying knapsacks and sticks have clearly got to the top without scaling the cliffs. This picture was used as a postcàrd in 1910 and the message reads: "Had a good time at Ambleside, although Newlands always takes the biscuit. This is our party on top of Great Gable pointing out to sea ". The 'party' is probably from the Co-operative Holidays Association (of which more on page 69) which had its roots in working class Lancashire and concentrated on walking holidays in preference to more expensive activities like rock climbing. 'Newlands' was the Association's first holiday centre opened in 1905.

The view down Wasdale from the top of Great Gable must have thrilled people who spent most of their lives in grimy urban surroundings; by turning 90° they could enjoy this view of Styhead Tarn and Great End too.

Gable, in the distance here between Bowness Knott on the left and Pillar, Steeple and Haycock on the right, combines to form a mountain backdrop to Ennerdale Water as seen from the jetty of the Angler's Inn. As its name implies, fishing was the main attraction for many who ventured to this most remote of the western lakes. Fishing is still popular, but the inn is no longer there as it was demolished in the 1960s when the level of the lake was raised to provide water for Whitehaven.

Ennerdale Lake, View from Anglers' Hotel, looking up Lake. 2099

J. 6. BUTTERMERE. THE RETURN.

Across the hills from Ennerdale are the twin lakes of Buttermere and Crummock Water. Between them is Buttermere village, a collection of farms and hotels overlooked by a delightful little church. One of the hotels, the Bridge, formerly the Victoria, can be seen behind this coach, with the old village school on the right. The picture was taken from the entrance to Syke Farm which provided the writer of the note on the lower picture with dinner in 1923 and still provides accommodation and refreshments today.

The pictures on these two pages appear to have been taken on two or possibly three visits of a family to their favourite spot on the shore of Crummock Water, the beautiful pebble beach beside the outflow of the River Cocker. Their boat is typical of those hired from Lake District hotels, with the oars pivoting on outboard thole pins, rather than rowlocks. Great Gable can just be seen in the distance to the right of Rannerdale Knotts, the prominent hill at the top of the lake, with High Crag, High Stile and Red Pike further to the right. The steep slope of Mellbreak is behind the tree where the children are posing in the bottom picture, opposite.

Crummock Water was a favourite with the more discerning Victorian and Edwardian tourists although the magic seems a little lost on the children, unless they are just fed up having their picture taken so often! Behind them are the lower slopes of Grasmoor.

Fishing for salmon and sea trout on the swiftly flowing rivers of the western Lakes has always been popular. Here an angler tries his luck on the River Cocker as it flows through Lorton Vale.

The "pride of Lorton Vale" is how Wordsworth described this handsome yew tree, tucked away behind the village hall in High Lorton. The hall was once the nineteenth century malthouse of Jennings Brewery, becoming the hall in 1910 when Jennings moved their operations to Cockermouth. The Whit Beck, at the back of the hall, is seen here flowing between the tree and a cottage called Yew Tree View. The tree also inspired the founder of Quakerism, George Fox, who stood beside it to preach to a crowd watched over by Cromwell's soldiers. It is now watched over by a telephone box that "stands single in the midst" of this view of the tree.

The confluence of the River Cocker with the River Derwent gives Cockermouth its name. This footbridge over the river links the town's South Street with Cocker Lane and the east bank of the river. The bridge is now a more substantial steel arch.

Although not in the National Park, Cockermouth's credentials for being regarded as part of the Lake District are impeccable, if for no other reason than as Wordsworth's birthplace. The family house, at the west end of Main Street is too distant however to be seen in this 1906 view of Main Street from the Cocker Bridge. On the left here is the old courthouse and on the right, behind the carriage, the Conservative Club. The distinctive clock tower, in the centre of the picture, which stood at the junction of Station Street has gone.

The awesome Honister Crag, here casting a menacing shadow across the valley floor behind these 1930s winter motorists, dominates the descent to Buttermere on the steep, winding road over Honister Pass. This road is not for the faint hearted, the prospect of parting company with it concentrates the mind wonderfully and banishes any delusions of driving competence. With roads like this, it is little wonder so many people walk when they come to the Lake District!

William Layland's Rigghead quarry was started in the 1860s. It was one of many quarries working the distinctive green slate high up on the crags above Honister Pass. Here one of Layland's carts is loaded with slates, but before roads had been improved sufficiently for wheeled vehicles the slate was moved by sledge or packhorse. It was shipped out of Ravenglass having been taken over the hills by a route which went past the western edge of Great Gable to Wasdale. It was known, after a local whisky smuggler, as 'Moses' Trod'.

Seatoller, at the southern end of Borrowdale, grew from being an isolated farm into a quarrying and mining community as those industries developed around it. The quarries were on Honister, behind it here to the right, and the mines were at Seathwaite to the left. Graphite, plumbago, or 'wadd' as it is known locally, was being mined above Seathwaite late in the sixteenth century and continued to be mined until the end of the nineteenth. It was the raw material that started Cumberland's famous pencil industry.

As the old industries faltered, Seatoller, as elsewhere in the Lake District, turned its attention to tourists, becoming a centre for walking and climbing. It was well placed for access to Great Gable up the old smuggler's route used by the slate sleds. Here the entrance hall of Seatoller House, littered with climbing gear, resembles that of the Wasdale Head Hotel. Seatoller House is still offering accommodation for tourists as it was in Mrs Honey's day.

The Bowder Stane, this huge rock lying at the base of a rocky hillside in Borrowdale, has been a tourist attraction for as long as tourists have been drawn to the Lake District. The ladder, now replaced by a more robust structure, gave them easy access to the top. However, the road up to the 'Stane' was steep and narrow in places and it must have been harder for this pony to get there than for the occupants of its trap to climb the ladder. The road is now just a footpath.

High in a hidden hillside valley, due east of the Bowder Stane, is the farm hamlet of Watendlath beside Watendlath Tarn. Despite its isolation, its closeness to Borrowdale and its large hotels has made it a favourite with visitors, like these ladies strolling across the little bridge.

Giving up a career in the city for a life in the wilds may be the dream of every bored insurance man, but self-styled 'Professor of Adventure', Millican Dalton, did it, and with a vengeance. He is seen here on the slopes of High Lodore Farm beside the comparatively civilised dwelling of a tent. He also lived in a cave by Castle Crag at the head of Borrowdale, a marked contrast in style to the three star Borrowdale Hotel below.

Here, the Borrowdale Hotel can be seen in the distance to the right; its neighbour, the Lodore Hotel, is on the left behind these two boaters at the edge of Derwentwater. Behind the Lodore Hotel is one of the most frequented attractions of the area, the Lodore Falls, a 90 foot waterfall on Watendlath Beck. It was made famous by the poet Southey, but unfortunately, in dry weather, it did not always match his vivid description of the "never ending, always descending" stream of water.

57. MOTORING IN LAKELAND. CLIMBING BUTTERMERE HAUSE.

People drive on today's crowded, high speed, road-raged highways out of necessity, or laziness. Few, like this 1920s couple, will don their coat and hat and fold down the roof of the old jalopy to go 'motoring' for the sheer pleasure of driving on the open road. To such adventurers a hill climb offered the greatest challenge. They checked the tyres, oil and water before pitting themselves and their machine against a challenge like Buttermere Hause (now called Newlands Hause) and prided themelves on a job well done if they reached the top without the radiator boiling over.

533. COACHING UP BUTTERMERE HAUSE
(ABRAHAMS' SERIES.)

In coaching days, reaching the top was a case of getting off and walking as these passengers are doing. They are 'enjoying' one of the most popular Lakeland coach tours, the Buttermere Round which went from Keswick through Borrowdale and over Honister Pass to Buttermere, returning by way of Newlands and Portinscale. One of the coaches appears to be helping a cyclist by carrying the bicycle – a favour that would be scorned by today's 'go anywhere' mountain bikers.

A climb up the 2000 foot Causey Pike can be the start of some wonderful ridge walks, but whether these walkers from the Holiday Fellowship are continuing on a longer walk or simply, as the original caption suggests, "climbing Causey" is anyone's guess. The Fellowship was formed in 1913, growing out of the earlier Co-operative Holidays Association which had been formed in 1897 to provide recreational and educational holidays. The Association converted an old mill at Stair in the Vale of Newlands into holiday accommodation. It was later taken over by the Holiday Fellowship and because Causey Pike was almost in its backyard, this walk must have been a favourite with generations of people staying at Newlands.

New houses, conversions and attic extensions have contrived to alter this view of Braithwaite, but not yet change it out of all recognition. The field on the right has been built on and the tree beside Laburnam House, the large house on the left, has gone to make way for another house. Pencils were once made in Braithwaite, but when the works burned down production was moved to Keswick.

The power for the Lodore and Derwentwater Hotels' electric launch *May Queen* is said to have been generated by the Lodore Falls. If true, she must score highly on any league table of 'green' boats, although providing power to the batteries in a dry season must have been difficult. She is seen here at the Keswick jetty with Derwent Island behind and the distinctive shape of Causey Pike is in the distance on the left, between the trees.

Causey Pike is in the distance here too as one of the Keswick boat hiring jetties provides a last refuge of terra firma for skaters uncertain of their skills. Although undated, the picture could, like that of Windermere on page 23, be from February 1907 when the sheet ice on Derwentwater was the most perfect remembered, smooth, hard and without a flake of snow on it. It was so good the railway ran skaters' specials from Carlisle.

Perhaps the same winter frost also inspired this evocative view of Crosthwaite Church from Church Lane. The church, on the western edge of Keswick is believed to have been founded in 553 A.D. by Saint Kentigern, patron saint of Glasgow. The present church, the fourth on the site, was built in the sixteenth century, incorporating parts of the fourteenth century building. Canon Hardwicke Rawnsley, one of the three co-founders of the National Trust, was vicar of Crosthwaite from 1888 to 1917.

This hump-back bridge over the River Greta to the west of Keswick was rebuilt in 1926 with flatter arches and less of a hump. To its right here is the mill which was taken over as a pencil mill in the mid-nineteenth century by Ann Banks, the widow of the town's principal pencil-maker Joseph Banks. The mill continued making pencils until production was moved to the works on the other side of the road. Pencils are still made there, continuing an industry that was established in Keswick in the sixteenth century. The full story is told at the excellent pencil museum beside the present works.

King Edward I granted Keswick its market charter in 1276 and there is still a Saturday market held in the town. Market stalls have been set up here in front of the Moot Hall in the centre of this view looking east along Main Street to Market Square. The present building replaced an earlier one in 1813 and has been in its time a market hall, court house, prison, museum and town hall. It is now used as the Tourist Information Centre. Tourism and pencil-making are the town's main industries now.

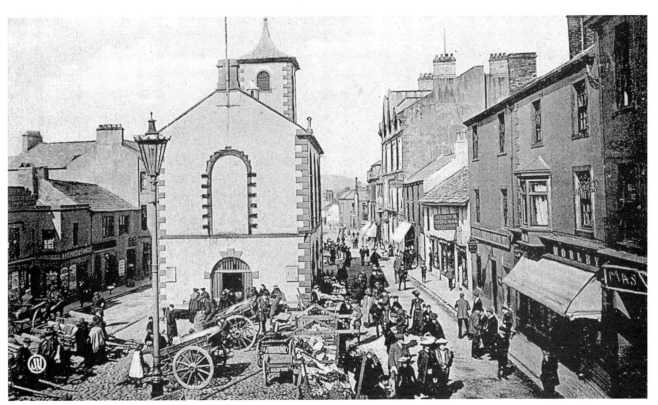

The arched entrance to the market hall in the east gable is now used by the Tourist Centre. Glass and varnished wood have replaced the wooden slats and the building itself looks very different as the whitewashed roughcast has been removed and the stonework exposed. An opening through the buildings on the right here leads to Packhorse Court, once one of many yards and alleys behind the street frontages crowded with small businesses. It is now a shopping precinct incorporating the National Trust's multi-media presentation, Beatrix Potter's Lake District.

Packhorse Court leads round into Station Street past the entrance to the Royal Oak Hotel. The hotel claimed to have been "the social and commercial centre of the town since Elizabethan times" and it was from here, before improvements were made to the turnpike roads, that packhorses left with the town's produce for the south. The building seen here dates from 1909 when it was owned by David Pape who also owned the coach and bus loading up outside.

For a time John George Hudson occupied these two shops at 2 and 4 St John Street for his fish monger and fruiterer's businesses, but later he concentrated solely on the fish shop. The shops have now been knocked into one and the facade lowered.

The National Westminster Bank now occupies the site at 28 Main Street where Fleming's grocery and provision stores once were. This advertising postcard of the shop and its staff is, according to the message on the back, actually meant as a picture of Willie – that's him marked with a cross.

Boot maker Frederick Birkett moved into number 2 St John Street, beside Hudson's fish shop. He made a climbing boot called the Keswick Boot and, as this advertising card shows, hired the eccentric Millican Dalton to 'model' them for him. The nails on the edge of the boot and defining the heel were known as Clinkers and the pattern on the sole was made up with three headed nails called Tricouni nails. They made a lot more noise than today's moulded composition soles.

Keswick was home to some of the finest early photographers in the country – Petit's of St John Street, Mayson's, whose 'emporium' in Lake Road still survives, and Abraham's on the corner of Lake Road and Borrowdale Road. That firm was founded in 1869 by George Abraham, but it was his sons George and Ashley that made a name for themselves as pioneers of mountain photography and their books and lectures did much to popularise mountaineering and rock climbing. This hand traverse shot is one of their pictures – the climber may even be wearing a pair of Keswick boots.

Thousands of trippers were attracted to the northern Lakes by the Cockermouth, Keswick and Penrith Railway when it opened for passengers in 1865. Despite the obvious mass appeal of the area, the company saw Keswick as a more exclusive middle-class resort than Windermere and to cater for this market built the 76 room Keswick Hotel with an entrance direct from the station. It was opened in 1869 and through its ties with the railway offered tours of northern Lakeland by rail and road; some of its large fleet of carriages are seen here setting off on various excursions.

Part of the ground for the Fitz Park was purchased from the Keswick Hotel which can be seen behind the trees to the right of this view of Upper Fitz Park. The park opened in 1887 having been funded by donations which were the result of a considerable effort by Henry Irwin Jenkinson, whose work is commemmorated by the main gates into the upper park. These are opposite the Keswick Museum and Art Gallery.

RICHARDSON'S ORIGINAL MUSICAL STONES IN KESWICK MUSEUM.

Rock music came to Keswick in 1785 when museum owner Peter Crosthwaite discovered the musical properties of stones gathered from the sand beds of the River Greta. He created a sixteen note set which he played to attract visitors to his private museum. Some years later Joseph Richardson, son of a Keswick stonemason, created this much larger set of 'original' musical stones called the rock, bell and steel band. Encouraged by a successful tour of the North of England, Richardson and his three sons took it to London where they played three times in front of Queen Victoria. Richardson's stones are now displayed at the Keswick Museum along with some exhibits from Peter Crosthwaite's old museum.

Keswick's hotels and boarding houses were usually filled during the week of the 'Convention' but in 1908, when this picture was taken, the lower than usual attendance coincided with a bad year for tourists. The town's hoteliers were worried. Their mood however was in marked contrast to the enthusiasm of the multinational, multi-faith Conventionalists who attended the usual variety of meetings and bible readings in the two large marquees in Eskin Street and Skiddaw Street.

Like the hut at Easedale Tarn this shack on the path up Skiddaw provided tourists with refreshments as they toiled up to the 3053 foot summit. Edwardian tourists had a more cavalier attitude to the mountains; the ladies' clothing here would certainly not be recommended today as suitable fell walking kit and you can be sure those voluminous dresses did not conceal a couple of well-worn pairs of Keswick boots.

Much more suitable for Edwardian ladies-wear was a simple stroll through the village of Applethwaite to the north of Keswick. Behind the village are the southern slopes of Skiddaw. This country village scene, with a dirt road weaving between cottages and farm buildings, is in marked contrast to the more manicured picture the place presents today.

Bassenthwaite Lake station was at the northern end of the lake, on the Cockermouth, Keswick and Penrith Railway which ran along the lake's western shore. When the line west of Keswick was closed in 1966 part of the track bed was used to improve the A66 road which passes close to these old station buildings, now rotting gently behind a screen of trees. The station house at the end of the left hand platform however, still survives. Beyond it, the road to Wythop Mill is no longer in danger of being held up by the level crossing gates.

The infant lime trees in this view across the large village green at Bassenthwaite have now grown to maturity, providing an elegant avenue for a village nestling below the huge bulk of Skiddaw. In this view, however, the photographer looks the other way towards the Uldale Fells.

Bassenthwaite, and the village of Uldale to the north, lie in rolling hill country 'back o' Skidda'. Uldale, seen here looking north across the village green, sits above the River Ellen on a cross roads from Ireby to Overwater and Bassenthwaite to Caldbeck. The road to Caldbeck is hidden by the houses on the right as it heads up the hill towards the church.

Binsey, the low hill seen here beyond the village, frames the spire of St John's Church beside the Caldbeck road as if to accept the typically Victorian, untypically Lakeland church into the landscape. The Lakeland weather however, disagreed with the building and it was demolished in 1963 when it became unsafe. The perimeter wall was left and now surrounds a tennis court and children's play park. Gates, like the one across the road in the foreground here, were once common impediments on Lakeland roads, but cattle grids now keep the traffic moving.

Caldbeck on the northern edge of the National Park was the home of England's most famous huntsman, John Peel. Immortalised in song, he was, despite wearing a "coat so grey", a colourful character, more often drunk than sober and who preferred horse dealing and hunting to family matters. He died in 1854 as a result of a hunting accident and is buried at Saint Kentigern's churchyard. The church is out of picture to the right of this view looking past the post office cum village store, to the Oddfellows Arms on the left.

One of the Lake District's eighty bobbin mills was at Caldbeck. It was sited at the mouth of a limestone gorge known as the Howk which has been carved into fantastic shapes by the beck that gives the town its name. The mill operated between 1857 and 1920 and was powered by a 42 foot diameter water wheel known as Auld Red Rover, shown here behind the mill.

With Skiddaw in the distance to the north, this coach has paused outside the old toll house at the top of Chestnut Hill (now the A591 road) on its way south out of Keswick to Thirlmere and beyond.

Thirlmere was two small lakes until Manchester Corporation dammed its outlet to create a reservoir for the city. It was inauguated in 1894. Fourteen years later, in June 1908, a three month old traction engine was towing two wagons from a travelling cinematograph show along the road above Thirlmere. Suddenly, it veered off the road and crashed down the embankment into the reservoir, killing the driver and stoker. The wagons it was towing were also smashed to pieces on the rocks but just as they left the road, the women and children travelling in them jumped to safety. Miraculously, they sustained only minor injuries and were taken to the King's Head Inn at Thirlspot to recover. Subsidence of the embankment was found to be the cause.

At the southern end of the valley, the village of Wythburn was a popular stopping place for the tourist coaches travelling between Keswick and the central lakes. This coach is outside the Nag's Head Inn. As seen here, it was still in business a few years after the reservoir was inaugurated, but was eventually forced to close as the waters rose around it. The site is now a small plantation. To the right of the coach is the boundary wall of Wythburn church, seen in the lower picture. It is a delightful little building that survived the flood but lost its congregation as one by one the surrounding community was forced out by the rising tide. The little church now stands alone, surrounded by a forest. Manchester Corporation stirred up even more controversy when they planted conifers on the steep sides of the valley to bind the soil and prevent it being washed into their new reservoir.

The Helvellyn range stands between Wythburn and Patterdale to the east. Patterdale is the name given to both the valley that runs down from Kirkstone Pass and the village at its northern end beside Ullswater. Lead has been mined in the hills around Patterdale from Elizabethan times but as the viable deposits dwindled and tourist numbers grew, Patterdale began to work that somewhat richer seam. One of the village tourist 'traps' was William Kilner's Tea Gardens, seen here across the road from St Patrick's Church.

Patterdale is named after St Patrick who is reputed to have come to Ullswater after being shipwrecked at Duddon Sands. He is believed to have baptised people at this 'holy well', known as St Patrick's Well, beside the lakeside road between Patterdale and Glenriddding. Roofed and elevated into a tourist attraction for the Ullswater coach parties, it appears to be an attraction here for a thirsty horse.

If tea on the lawn was one popular aspect of Edwardian tourism, another was the picture postcard. Here a party from the Wesleyan Methodist Chapel of Union Street, Carlisle, relax beside the hut that served as a picture postcard shop, although this particular postcard was taken by a Carlisle photographer who presumably went to Patterdale with the Methodists.

Postcards appear to be the main attraction here too at Glenridding with a prominent display outside the shop on the right. A glass awning now covers the much reduced footpath. Milcrest's Hotel on the left here, now the Glenridding Hotel, advertised itself as a first class private hotel commanding extensive views of lake and mountain. Mining was still part of Glenridding life up to 1962 when the Greenside Mine, one of the best lead deposits in England, was finally exhausted.

The Ullswater Navigation and Transit Co. Ltd operated steamer services on the lake from Glenridding Pier to Howtown and Pooley Bridge. Their two steamers were *Lady of the Lake*, built in 1877, and *Raven* built in sections in 1889 by Seath's of Rutherglen and reassembled on the lake shore. They are seen here at Glenridding; *Raven* is pictured above. They were both converted to diesel in the 1930s and despite a fire on *Lady of the Lake* in the 1960s are still operating today.

Many people regard Ullswater as the most beautiful of the lakes; it was of course where Wordsworth saw his "host of golden daffodils", so often used as a Lake District symbol. A journey along its length, be it by steamer or by car is to experience a rich variety of scenery from the high southern mountains to the gently rolling northern hills. The National Trust's Gowbarrow Park on the western side includes Aira Force, one of Lakeland's highest waterfalls.

Pooley Bridge is set back from the northern end of Ullswater and so its pier is a short distance from the village, close to the mouth of the River Eamont. Here a coach and charabanc have met up with one of the lake steamers which has come in to the pier.

The river crossing at Pooley Bridge has clearly been of strategic importance for centuries. Guarding it, on the hill overlooking the bridge, is a hill fort with an old Celtic name, Dunmallet. More recently the old county boundary between Cumberland and Westmorland, which ran down the middle of Ullswater, also split the River Eamont and so the bridge here spanned two counties. A 10 mph speed limit is now imposed on Ullswater, a speed these low technology hire boats would have difficulty reaching, let alone breaking.

This picture postcard, was sent to a Mrs McTavish in Edinburgh by her son who was staying at the hotel. McTavish was a cricketer and his team, Royal High School former pupils, thrashed a weakened Penrith team and went on the following day to trounce Kirkby Stephen – McTavish scoring a century! No doubt these were friendlier encounters than the Scottish raids that once ravaged the town!

King Street in Penrith, 'the gateway to the North' clogged with carts in the days before it was clogged by motor vehicles. On the left, beyond the grocers Pears and Elliott's who were "... noted for Cumberland hams and bacon", is the Herald office, while on the extreme right is Reed's who sold, amongst other things the picture postcard of the boy on the opposite page.

Ten year old Thomas Victor Martindale from Penrith, became, briefly, a local celebrity when he went missing on the Bampton fells in late July 1907. He was staying at High How farm and had gone on to the hills with the farmer's son to look for a pony, but the two boys became separated in thick mist on Loadpot Hill. From there Martindale made his way across Nan Bield to Kentmere Reservoir where he was given directions back. He set off again over Nan Bield, but, at the top of the pass, instead of turning for Mardale he went left towards High Street and four days and nights of loneliness and hunger. With only water from the becks to sustain him he spent the days wandering in the mist and the nights in what shelter he could find until he came across a field of cows where he waited for the farmer, and rescue. This was at Troutbeck Park near Windermere, and here he is footsore, hungry and happy to be alive!

During his ordeal young Martindale must have longed for home comforts, discovering, on his second night, what 'home comforts' mean for sheep. He curled up in the shelter of one of those sheep-worn hillside hollows where he was joined by a lamb. It apparently kept him warm through the night, but ran away in the morning, no doubt surprised to wake up and find an alien sharing its bedroom. The dominant local breed is the Herdwick, a hardy, agile animal with coarse, hairy wool and ideally suited to a life on the fells. It is probably descended from an old Norse breed of sheep and not, as one popular theory suggests, from animals that escaped from a wrecked ship of the Spanish Armada.

The image of sheep munching grass and wandering contentedly over the fells belies the long hours of hard work by hill shepherds to look after their flocks. The top picture shows sheep on the lower slopes of Fairfield being dipped to rid them of parasites, while below, in a seemingly less hectic activity, they are being clipped.

Sheep, like small boys, can get lost too and throughout the Lake District there were and indeed still are meeting places where the hill shepherds gathered to sort out the ownership of sheep that had strayed from their flock. One such meeting place was the Dun Bull Hotel at Mardale. It had originally been a farmhouse inn catering for travellers on the road that led over the Gatescarth and Nan Bield Passes to Kendal. Its early reputation fluctuated somewhat with travellers being advised that it was either a comfortable inn or a place to be avoided.

Gatescarth Pass is seen on the right here above the much extended hotel early in the twentieth century. With the advent of wheeled vehicles the roads, which were narrow and suitable only for horses or pedestrians, fell into disuse. Mardale became a cul-de-sac and the Dun Bull was at the end of the road.

Mardale's isolation was also its undoing, because Manchester Corporation, since its earlier flooding of Thirlmere, had continued to look for exploitable water in the Lake District – they found it in remote Haweswater. When the Haweswater Act was passed through Parliament in 1919 Mardale's fate was sealed. Farms, hotel and school were all to be flooded along with the little church, seen here nestling amongst its yew trees with Rough Crag and High Street Ridge behind.

The church sat between Riggindale Beck and Mardale Beck across the old road from Chapel Hill Farm. It was originally a simple seventeenth century building, typical of the smaller Lakeland churches like Wythburn although its external appearance had been altered by the addition of a square battlemented tower. Now it was all to be demolished, although, acceding to a request from the Bishop of Carlisle, it was dismantled stone by stone, rather than being blown up. The stones were used to build the reservoir draw-off tower.

Some of the other fittings found new homes at other churches. The weather vane was re-sited on the church tower at Shap, and the bell, dating from 1825, and many other fittings went to the new St Barnabus' church in Carlisle. The pulpit went to Rosthwaite in Borrowdale and the pews were made into seats for the new Haweswater Hotel. One hundred and four bodies were disinterred from the churchyard and most were reburied in a corner of the graveyard at Shap.

Like the much bigger St Oswald's at Grasmere, the plain unadorned exterior of the Mardale church belied an attractive interior of oak pulpit, screen, altar rails and gallery. Its pews, also made of oak, normally seated 50 people, but on the 18th of August 1935, 75 ticket holders crowded in to hear the Bishop of Carlisle conduct the last service. Thousands more gathered outside to hear the service relayed on loudspeakers despite inclement weather.

The largest hollow buttress dam in the world was built to hold back the waters of Haweswater Beck and create the reservoir. It was a feat of engineering overshadowed by the emotion surrounding its construction. Work started in 1930, but was halted during the depression years of 1931 to 1934. However, it was in full swing when this picture was taken in 1937 and the dam was complete and ready for use in 1941.

The dam raised the level of the lake by 96 feet and increased it in length from two and a half to four miles, covering this gently sloping valley floor. The old road, on the west side of the lake and seen here near its head, was replaced by a new one carved out of the hillside opposite. Halfway along it and eighty feet above the water line, Manchester Corporation built the Haweswater Hotel to replace the old Dun Bull – Mardale had disappeared.

During periods of drought, however, Mardale reappears to remind new generations of past follies. This picture, with the ruins of the Dun Bull in the foreground, was taken in 1995 when people poured into the valley from miles around to clog up the dead end road and turn the drowned village into a tourist attraction sixty years after it died. The conspicuous rectangle, to the left of centre, is believed to have been the hotel's tennis court. In the final years the Dun Bull catered for visiting climbers, fishermen and walkers and for local people too.

In 1885 sixty-four guests came to the funeral dinner of Hugh Parker Holme at the Dun Bull. He was the last of the male line of Mardale's most prominent family, the Holme's, known as the 'Kings' of Mardale. The last female member of the family was Mary Holme, a great benefactor to the village, who died in 1915, thus ensuring that none of the Holme's survived to see the end of their kingdom.

ACKNOWLEDGEMENTS

Maybe I have been lucky, but I have yet to meet a grumpy Cumbrian. This has been a major factor in making the compilation of this book a real pleasure and I must therefore thank the many people who I have bumped into on my travels for their kindness and their help. I must thank in particular Jane and Tony Chambers for their considerable help with the pictures. I must thank too Ashley Kendal and John Alsop who also helped by supplying pictures and John Dickson of Hawkshead Heritage who supplied the story of the 'great clog'. The libraries in Carlisle, Penrith and Kendal also proved to be fertile ground in the hunt for 'stories' as did the pubs, shops and farms where I asked for help.

The other delight has been the opportunity to travel around this beautiful countryside in the off-season, when it has not only been quiet but when the autumn leaves have been in spectacular hue and the winter snows set against cloudless skies have been breathtaking. To the people and the place – thankyou

Backbarrow Methodist Church, 1906.

Richard Stenlake Publishing has a wide range of local history and transport books in print.
For more information and a current catalogue,
please write to:

**Richard Stenlake Publishing, Ochiltree Sawmill, The Lade,
Ochiltree, Ayrshire, KA18 2NX
Telephone: 01290 423114**